AstroHerbology

AstroHerbology

Volume 1

Matthew Petchinsky

Apophis Enterprises LLC

AstroHerbology: The Sky and The Soil

AstroHerbology: The Sky and The Soil: Volume 1
By Matthew Petchinsky

<u>Introduction 1A</u>

Astrology has been a fascination for thousands of years, there are many different versions of it and it has had the hearts and mind of man in every culture on Earth, since mankind was primitive Caveman in a cave to Egyptian to modern man. Astrology is engrained in our DNA. Please enjoy this book.

Introduction: The Convergence of Cosmos and Earth

AstroHerbology represents a unique and enchanting intersection where the vastness of the cosmos meets the nurturing bosom of the Earth. This intricate convergence is not a modern concept but rather a revival and renaissance of ancient wisdom where celestial mechanics and terrestrial life intermingle, influencing and enriching each other. The practice of AstroHerbology, though sounding novel to the uninitiated, is deeply rooted in the age-old traditions that observed and revered the dance between the skies and the soil. This book, "AstroHerbology: The Sky and The Soil," aims to unravel these complex relationships, offering a comprehensive guide that charts the influences of celestial bodies on terrestrial flora, and explores how these powerful dynamics can be harnessed to enhance both personal well-being and planetary health.

AstroHerbology Explained: Defining the Practice and Its Historical Roots

AstroHerbology is an interdisciplinary practice that synthesizes the ancient art of herbalism with the science of astrology. It is predicated on the belief that plants, like all entities on Earth, are influenced by the gravitational and energetic forces exerted by celestial bodies—particularly the sun, moon, and planets. Historically, practitioners from diverse cultures, including the ancient Babylonians, Greeks, Chinese, and Native Americans, observed the positions of celestial bodies to determine the most auspicious times for planting, harvesting, and utilizing plants for medicinal purposes.

This section of the book delves into the rich tapestry of AstroHerbology's past, exploring how different civilizations understood and applied these cosmic influences. It discusses how ancient texts and archaeological findings support the existence of such practices, and how modern AstroHerbologists are rediscovering and validating these traditional methods through both empirical evidence and intuitive practice.

The Celestial Influence: Overview of How Celestial Bodies Influence Plant Growth and Potency

The celestial influence on plant life is both subtle and profound. The cycles of the moon, the position of the planets, and the sun's journey through the zodiac are believed to affect various aspects of plant growth and development. For instance, lunar phases are thought to influence sap flow and root development, with different phases being optimal for specific gardening activities. Similarly, planetary alignments are considered to influence plant potency and effectiveness, especially in medicinal and ritual uses.

This chapter provides a detailed exploration of the mechanisms by which celestial bodies are believed to impact plants. It covers the scientific underpinnings where available, such as studies on lunar gravitropism, and blends these findings with anecdotal and historical perspectives that have guided traditional practices. The discussion extends to practical guidance on how to observe celestial phenomena and apply this knowledge in gardening and herbal medicine preparation.

Navigating the Book: How Readers Can Use the Book to Enhance Their Understanding and Practice of AstroHerbology

"AstroHerbology: The Sky and The Soil" is structured to be both a reference and a guide. To get the most out of this book, readers are encouraged to approach it not just as a source of information, but as a tool for personal and ecological transformation. Each chapter is designed to build upon the last, gradually deepening the reader's understanding of how celestial dynamics influence terrestrial life and how these influences can be applied for healing and growth.

This section outlines the book's layout, explaining how each chapter connects to the next and suggesting ways to integrate the knowledge into daily practice. It provides practical tips on how to use the book's calendars and diagrams, which map out celestial events and their corresponding herbal activities. Additionally, it encourages readers to keep a personal journal of their AstroHerbological observations and experiments, fostering a deeper, experiential connection with the material.

Through this introduction and the chapters that follow, "AstroHerbology: The Sky and The Soil" invites readers on a journey that not only educates but also empowers, offering a pathway to living in deeper harmony with the natural world by understanding the cosmic forces that animate it.

Chapter 1: Foundations of AstroHerbology

In the realm of AstroHerbology, the knowledge of the cosmos and the earth are intertwined, each enriching the understanding and application of the other. This chapter lays the essential groundwork for novices and seasoned practitioners alike, bridging gaps between two disciplines: astrology and herbology. By establishing a solid foundation in these areas, we provide readers with the tools to explore the deeper connections between celestial influences and plant life, essential for practicing AstroHerbology.

Astrological Basics for Gardeners

For gardeners with a robust understanding of herbology but who might be new to astrology, this section serves as an essential introduction. Astrology, in the context of gardening, involves understanding how the movements and positions of celestial bodies like the sun, moon, and planets influence plant growth and development.

Key Concepts:

- **Zodiac Signs:** There are twelve zodiac signs, each associated with specific elemental energies (Earth, Water, Air, Fire) and modalities (Cardinal, Fixed, Mutable) that influence plant characteristics.
- **Lunar Phases:** The moon's cycle from new to full and back again affects moisture absorption and root growth. Planting, pruning, and harvesting activities can be optimized by aligning them with lunar phases.
- **Planetary Aspects:** The angular relationships between planets (such as conjunctions, squares, and oppositions) can suggest optimal times for certain gardening activities.

Application in Gardening:

- Using lunar calendars to plan gardening activities.
- Observing planetary hours for planting medicinal herbs.
- Aligning crop rotations with solar ingress into zodiac signs.

Herbology Basics for Astrologers

For astrologers keen to deepen their understanding of herbology, this section provides a foundational primer. Herbology, or the study and use of plants for medicinal and culinary purposes, requires an understanding of plant biology, ecology, and the medicinal properties of herbs.

Key Concepts:

- **Plant Anatomy:** Knowledge of plant parts (roots, stems, leaves, flowers) and their functions is crucial for identifying and harvesting the correct part of the herb.
- **Plant Properties:** Each plant possesses unique properties that can be used to treat specific ailments or enhance well-being. These properties include but are not limited to, aromatic, culinary, medicinal, and toxic.
- **Harvesting and Storage:** Techniques for harvesting, drying, and storing herbs to maintain their potency.

Application in Astrology:

- Choosing the right plants for creating astrologically themed remedies.
- Understanding how planetary influences can enhance the efficacy of herbal preparations.
- Using herbs to balance elemental energies in natal charts or during challenging astrological transits.

The Zodiac and Plant Correspondences

This section delves into the fascinating correspondences between the zodiac signs and plant characteristics, which is central to practicing AstroHerbology. Each zodiac sign imparts different energies to plants through its elemental (Earth, Air, Fire, Water) and modal (Cardinal, Fixed, Mutable) qualities.

Elemental and Modal Qualities:

- **Fire Signs (Aries, Leo, Sagittarius):** Plants associated with these signs often thrive in hot conditions and may have invigorating, warming properties.
- **Earth Signs (Taurus, Virgo, Capricorn):** These plants typically require stability and can be grounding, often used for their nutritional values and sturdy medicinal properties.
- **Air Signs (Gemini, Libra, Aquarius):** Associated plants may favor lighter soils and have benefits for the respiratory system or nervous system, promoting communication and intellect.
- **Water Signs (Cancer, Scorpio, Pisces):** These plants often thrive in moist conditions and can have soothing, cleansing, and emotional healing properties.

Zodiac-Plant Associations:

- Detailed tables and charts in this section list plants associated with each zodiac sign, explaining the reasoning behind these associations based on traditional correspondences in mythology, folklore, and astrological lore.

By understanding these foundational concepts, readers of "Astro-Herbology: The Sky and The Soil" are equipped to explore the deeper interplay between the alignment of the stars and the growth of plants on Earth. This knowledge not only enhances the practical aspects of gardening and herbalism but also enriches the spiritual and holistic connection to the natural world.

If you want to see some amazing products, please visit my Virtual Dispensary: https://shift.store/sg1fan23477/retail

Chapter 2: Aries and the Fire of Germination

Aries, the first sign of the zodiac, is characterized by its cardinal fire energy, which instills a pioneering and initiatory force. This chapter explores how the vigorous and fiery nature of Aries influences the growth and use of certain herbs. These plants, imbued with the spirit of Aries and ruled by Mars, possess unique qualities that make them vital in both practical and esoteric practices. Here, we explore the characteristics of Aries herbs, provide guidance on cultivating these powerful plants, and delve into their varied uses in medicine and magic.

Aries Herbs Overview: Characteristics of Herbs Ruled by Aries and Their Fiery Qualities

Herbs associated with Aries typically share certain fiery characteristics: they are often pioneers in their ecosystems, first to emerge in spring, and may possess sharp, spicy, or warming flavors and medicinal properties. These herbs are energizers, capable of stirring up both physical and mental activity, and often support courage, initiative, and action.

Key Aries Herbs:

- **Nettle:** This herb embodies the aggressive warrior spirit of Mars with its stinging leaves, which, when processed correctly, are rich in nutrients and vitality.
- **Basil:** Known for its sharp and peppery flavor, basil stimulates warmth and circulation, reflecting the passionate nature of Aries.

- **Mustard:** With its potent heat, mustard promotes vigor and stimulates metabolism, echoing the dynamic Aries energy.

These herbs not only grow with a strong and assertive force but also impart these qualities through their culinary and medicinal uses.

Cultivating Aries Herbs: Tips for Planting and Nurturing Aries-associated Herbs, Considering Mars' Influence

Growing Aries herbs requires understanding the influence of Mars, which governs energy, action, and conflict. This martial influence can be harnessed to cultivate these herbs successfully by recognizing their need for certain conditions to thrive.

Cultivation Tips:

- **Sun Exposure:** Aries herbs generally require full sun to mimic the fiery energy they embody. Ensure they receive at least 6-8 hours of direct sunlight daily.
- **Soil Conditions:** These herbs do well in well-drained soil that mimics the dry conditions often preferred by Mars-ruled plants. Adding sand or small pebbles can improve drainage.
- **Germination:** Aries herbs often germinate quickly and like to be the first to break soil in early spring. Sowing seeds as soon as the soil can be worked reflects their pioneering nature.

Planting and tending to these herbs during Mars hours of the day (first and eighth hours after sunrise) can further align your gardening practices with astrological energies, enhancing growth and potency.

Aries Herb Uses and Rituals: Medicinal and Magical Uses of Aries Herbs, Including Recipes and Rituals for Harnessing Their Energetic Properties

Aries herbs are not just culinary delights but also powerful medicinal and magical allies. Their fiery nature makes them perfect for use in boosting energy, protecting against illness, and conducting rituals that invoke courage and protection.

Medicinal Uses:

- **Nettle:** Used in teas or tinctures, nettle can detoxify the blood and stimulate the metabolism, providing an energetic boost.
- **Basil:** This herb can alleviate digestive discomfort and improve mood, reflecting its uplifting Mars qualities.
- **Mustard:** Applied externally in plasters, mustard can relieve muscular pain and stiffness, showcasing its ability to stimulate and heal.

Magical Uses and Rituals:

- **Protection Spell:** Burn dried basil leaves to cleanse the home of negative energy and protect its inhabitants, invoking the protective spirit of Aries.
- **Courage Elixir:** Blend nettle tea with a pinch of cayenne and a few drops of ginger juice to create an elixir that bolsters courage and vitality before engaging in challenging endeavors.

Recipes:

- **Aries Fire Tonic:** A stimulating tonic can be made by infusing apple cider vinegar with Aries herbs like garlic (another Mars plant), basil, and mustard seeds. Let it steep for a month, then use it to boost immunity and energy.

Through these practices, "AstroHerbology: The Sky and The Soil" invites readers to embrace the robust and spirited energy of Aries in their gardening and herbal craft, using these dynamic herbs to ignite the fire within and revitalize both body and spirit.

If you want to see some amazing products, please visit my Virtual Dispensary: https://shift.store/sg1fan23477/retail

Chapter 3: Taurus and the Earth's Bounty

Taurus, ruled by Venus, is synonymous with fertility, stability, and the riches of the earth. This zodiac sign governs over growth that is slow but steady, reflecting the reliable and enduring qualities of the earth element. The herbs associated with Taurus possess these same bountiful and nurturing attributes, offering a wealth of benefits that extend from nutritional to medicinal and spiritual. This chapter explores the verdant world of Taurus herbs, provides advice on cultivating them in harmony with their Venusian influence, and discusses their uses in rituals aimed at enhancing grounding, fertility, and prosperity.

Taurus Herbs Overview: Exploring the Rich, Fertile Nature of Taurus and Its Herbs

Herbs ruled by Taurus are often those that thrive in rich, well-cultivated soil and tend to have strong, enduring qualities. They are typically lush, aromatic, and often have a soothing effect on both the body and the mind, reflecting the gentle influence of Venus.

Key Taurus Herbs:

- **Mint:** Known for its vigorous growth, mint is a hardy perennial that can thrive in many environments, symbolizing Taurus' love for stability and abundance.
- **Thyme:** This herb requires minimal intervention once established, representing Taurus' endurance and persistence.
- **Rose:** A symbol of Venus, roses are prized for their beauty and aromatic qualities, embodying the sensual and luxurious nature of Taurus.

These herbs are not only a testament to the fertility of the earth but also to the nurturing care that Taurus imparts to all growing things.

Cultivating Taurus Herbs: Guidance on Earth-Friendly Practices for Growing Taurus Herbs, Aligned with Venus' Influence

Cultivating Taurus herbs calls for practices that enhance and preserve the natural fertility of the earth, in line with Venus' attributes of beauty, pleasure, and sustainability.

Cultivation Tips:

- **Soil Preparation:** Taurus herbs flourish in rich, loamy soil. Amending your garden beds with compost and organic matter will mimic the fertile conditions these plants love.
- **Watering Practices:** These herbs generally require consistent moisture to thrive, reflecting Taurus' preference for stability and routine. Implementing a regular watering schedule helps mimic this consistency.
- **Plant Placement:** Venus' influence on Taurus emphasizes the beauty and harmony of the surroundings. Plant Taurus herbs in aesthetically pleasing arrangements and consider their sensory impact on the garden space.

Using biodynamic farming methods, which take into account astrological timings and lunar cycles, can also resonate well with the growth of Taurus herbs, enhancing their vitality and your connection to Venus.

Taurus Herb Uses and Rituals: Utilizing Taurus Herbs for Grounding, Fertility, and Prosperity Rituals

Taurus herbs are not only useful for their culinary and health benefits but also hold significant power in rituals related to grounding, fertility, and attracting prosperity—key themes governed by Taurus and Venus.

Grounding and Fertility Rituals:

- **Mint Meditation:** Chew fresh mint leaves or sip mint tea while meditating to enhance physical and spiritual grounding.
- **Thyme Fertility Charm:** Carry a sachet filled with thyme to promote fertility and strengthen your connection with the Earth's nurturing energies.

Prosperity Rituals:

- **Rose Prosperity Spell:** Petals of roses can be used in baths or as part of a sachet to attract abundance and pleasure. As you use them, visualize your desires manifesting with the help of Venus' abundant energy.
- **Herbal Prosperity Mix:** Create a mix of Taurus herbs, such as mint, thyme, and rose petals, and sprinkle it around your home or in your wallet to attract wealth and stability.

Recipes:

- **Taurus Herbal Butter:** Blend softened butter with minced Taurus herbs like thyme and mint for a spread that brings the grounding and enriching energies of Taurus to any meal.
- **Rose Syrup:** Simmer rose petals in water with sugar to create a syrup that captures the essence of Venus. Use it to sweeten teas or desserts, infusing them with Venusian qualities of pleasure and satisfaction.

Through these practices, "AstroHerbology: The Sky and The Soil" enables readers to harness the fertile and sustaining power of Taurus, grounding them in the richness of the Earth and opening paths to abundance and well-being.

If you want to see some amazing products, please visit my Virtual Dispensary: https://shift.store/sg1fan23477/retail

Chapter 4: Gemini and the Air of Communication

Gemini, ruled by Mercury, is synonymous with communication, intellect, and versatility. This mutable air sign influences a unique group of herbs that embody these qualities, enhancing cognitive functions and facilitating communication. This chapter explores the properties of Gemini-associated herbs, offers advice on cultivating them under the influence of Gemini's airy and mutable nature, and discusses their uses in rituals and recipes designed to boost mental clarity and enhance communication.

Gemini Herbs Overview: Herbs Associated with Gemini and Their Communicative Properties

Herbs that resonate with Gemini tend to support the nervous system, enhance cognitive functions, and aid in communication. These herbs often have light, airy qualities and are versatile in their uses, mirroring Gemini's adaptable and intellectual nature.

Key Gemini Herbs:

- **Lavender:** Known for its calming and soothing effects on the mind, lavender enhances communication by relieving anxiety and facilitating clearer thinking.
- **Lemon Balm:** This herb is reputed to improve mood and cognitive function, reflecting Mercury's influence on mental clarity and effective communication.
- **Parsley:** Often used to freshen breath, parsley also has a long-standing association with communication through its use in verbal eloquence and protection spells.

These herbs not only support mental functions but also encourage the fluidity and ease of expression characteristic of Gemini.

Cultivating Gemini Herbs: Techniques for Cultivating Herbs under Gemini's Mutable Air Influence

Growing herbs under the influence of Gemini's mutable air requires an understanding of the sign's need for variety and adaptability. These herbs often thrive in conditions that mimic Gemini's airy qualities.

Cultivation Tips:

- **Air Circulation:** Ensure that Gemini herbs are planted in areas with good air flow. This prevents fungal diseases and reflects the airy nature of Gemini.
- **Soil Type:** Light, well-draining soil is crucial for these herbs, mimicking the lightness of air. Incorporating sand or perlite can improve drainage and aeration.
- **Container Gardening:** Many Gemini herbs do well in containers, which allows for moving the plants to optimize conditions and satisfies Gemini's love for change.

Implementing companion planting can also be beneficial, as it supports the Gemini theme of connectivity and interaction, encouraging a symbiotic relationship among the garden plants.

Gemini Herb Uses and Rituals: Enhancing Communication and Cognitive Function Using Gemini Herbs, Including Recipes for Teas and Incenses

Gemini herbs are particularly effective in enhancing communication skills and boosting mental acuity, making them ideal for use in various cognitive and communicative rituals.

Cognitive and Communication Rituals:

- **Lavender Communication Spell:** Burn lavender incense before meetings or speeches to clear the mind and promote articulate communication.
- **Lemon Balm Tea Ritual:** Sip lemon balm tea while studying or before discussions to enhance memory and ease nervous tension.

Recipes:

- **Gemini Tea Blend:** Combine dried lavender, lemon balm, and a pinch of parsley in a tea infuser. Steep in hot water for a soothing tea that improves clarity and calms the mind.
- **Mercury Incense:** Create an incense blend using dried lavender, mint (another Mercury-ruled herb), and a bit of gum arabic as a base. Burn this incense when performing tasks that require concentration and clear communication.

Uses in Daily Practice:

- **Herbal Sachets:** Carry a small sachet filled with Gemini herbs like parsley and mint to facilitate eloquence and mental agility throughout the day.
- **Herbal Gargles:** Use a parsley and mint decoction as a gargle to freshen breath and enhance vocal clarity before important conversations.

Through these practices, "AstroHerbology: The Sky and The Soil" provides readers with the tools to harness the intellectual and communicative power of Gemini, enhancing mental agility and easing the flow of expression in everyday life. This not only fosters personal growth but also enhances interpersonal interactions by imbuing them with Mercury's clarity and dynamism.

If you want to see some amazing products, please visit my Virtual Dispensary: https://shift.store/sg1fan23477/retail

Chapter 5: Cancer and the Waters of Nurturance

Cancer, ruled by the Moon, is the zodiac sign deeply associated with emotions, family, and the nurturing aspect of water. This sign influences a variety of herbs that are imbued with protective and soothing qualities, resonating with Cancer's focus on care, emotional healing, and the safeguarding of home and family. This chapter delves into the characteristics of herbs associated with Cancer, offers guidelines for cultivating them in tune with Cancer's lunar and watery nature, and explores their uses in rituals designed to enhance emotional wellbeing and protection.

Cancer Herbs Overview: Herbs that Resonate with Cancer's Nurturing, Watery Nature

Herbs associated with Cancer are typically those that thrive in moist environments and have strong connections to the nurturing of the body and soul. They often have protective qualities and are used in healing, particularly in soothing emotional disturbances and enhancing familial bonds.

Key Cancer Herbs:

- **Chamomile:** Known for its calming effects, chamomile soothes the nervous system and aids in emotional distress, reflecting Cancer's nurturing qualities.
- **White Willow:** Often used in healing, the bark of the white willow helps relieve physical pain, which can be emotionally soothing, embodying Cancer's protective and caring traits.
- **Aloe Vera:** With its soothing gel, aloe vera is perfect for healing skin irritations and burns, symbolizing the Cancerian emphasis on care and nurture.

These herbs not only support physical and emotional health but also create an environment of comfort and security, reflecting the essence of Cancer.

Cultivating Cancer Herbs: Tips for Water-wise Gardening and Moon Phase Planting for Cancer Herbs

Cultivating Cancer-associated herbs requires an understanding of their need for stable, moist conditions, and the influence of lunar phases on their growth and potency.

Cultivation Tips:

- **Moisture Levels:** Cancer herbs thrive in well-watered gardens but also need proper drainage to prevent root rot. Implementing a drip irrigation system can provide consistent moisture while conserving water.
- **Moon Phase Planting:** Aligning planting activities with the phases of the moon can enhance the growth and medicinal qualities of Cancer herbs. New Moon is ideal for planting or sowing seeds, while the Full Moon is perfect for harvesting, especially for herbs used in healing and protective rituals.
- **Shade Requirements:** Many Cancer herbs benefit from partial shade, which mimics their natural understory or marshy habitats, providing a protective environment from the harshness of full sun.

Using mulch around these plants can help maintain moisture levels and protect the roots, which is particularly resonant with Cancer's protective nature.

Cancer Herb Uses and Rituals: Emotional Healing and Protective Uses of Cancer Herbs, with a Focus on Home and Family

Cancer herbs are particularly potent in rituals and remedies that focus on emotional healing, protection, and the enhancement of familial relationships.

Emotional Healing and Protection Rituals:

- **Chamomile Calming Bath:** Steep chamomile in a hot bath to create a soothing ritual that calms the mind and nurtures the body, ideal for easing emotional turmoil and fostering self-care.
- **White Willow Protection Amulet:** Create an amulet using white willow bark for protection against pain and negativity; keep it in the home to shield family members from harm.
- **Aloe Vera Home Blessing Gel:** Use aloe vera gel mixed with protective herbs like rosemary to anoint windows and doorways, protecting the home from negative influences and enhancing the comfort and safety of its inhabitants.

Recipes:

- **Cancer Soothing Tea:** Blend chamomile, mint, and lemon balm to create a tea that helps relieve stress and anxiety, promoting emotional well-being and a sense of familial harmony.
- **Healing Salve:** Combine infused oils from Cancer herbs such as white willow and aloe vera with beeswax to create a salve that can be used to heal cuts, burns, and bruises, offering physical and emotional relief.

Through these practices, "AstroHerbology: The Sky and The Soil" empowers readers to harness the deeply nurturing and protective energies of Cancer, fostering emotional balance and safeguarding the sanctity of home and family life. This not only promotes personal healing but also enhances the communal and familial bonds that are central to Cancer's spirit.

If you want to see some amazing products, please visit my Virtual Dispensary: https://shift.store/sg1fan23477/retail

Chapter 6: Leo and the Fire of Creativity

Leo, ruled by the Sun, embodies warmth, creativity, and confidence. This sign influences a range of herbs that resonate with Leo's bold, radiant energy. These herbs often possess heart-strengthening and confidence-boosting properties, reflecting Leo's regal and vivacious character. This chapter explores the distinctive traits of Leo-associated herbs, provides guidance on how to cultivate them under the influence of the Sun, and delves into their uses in rituals aimed at enhancing creativity, boosting performance, and strengthening the heart and spirit.

Leo Herbs Overview: Herbs Ruled by Leo and Their Uses in Boosting Creativity and Confidence

Herbs associated with Leo are vibrant and often have properties that support vitality, heart health, and self-expression. These plants are not only physically striking but also have robust flavors and aromas that can invigorate the spirit and spark creativity.

Key Leo Herbs:

- **Sunflower:** Symbolic of the Sun itself, sunflowers are not only visually striking but their seeds are rich in nutrients that support heart health and vitality.
- **Calendula:** Known for its bright, sunny flowers, calendula is beneficial for skin health and promotes overall vitality, embodying the Sun's life-giving energy.
- **Saffron:** A spice associated with luxury and vitality, saffron is used for its mood-enhancing properties, helping to elevate the spirit and inspire creativity.

These herbs align with Leo's flamboyant nature and its association with the heart, both physically and metaphorically.

Cultivating Leo Herbs: Insights into the Sun-soaked Cultivation of Leo-associated Herbs

Cultivating Leo herbs requires an environment that mimics the Sun's warmth and brightness, essential for imbuing these plants with their full potential energy and vigor.

Cultivation Tips:

- **Sun Exposure:** Leo herbs thrive in full sun, requiring several hours of direct sunlight daily to develop their vibrant colors and medicinal properties.
- **Soil Conditions:** These herbs prefer well-drained soil that stays moderately moist but not waterlogged. Adding organic matter will help keep the soil fertile and airy.
- **Spacing and Support:** Sunflowers and other tall Leo herbs may need space to spread and supports to help them grow upright, reflecting Leo's need for space to showcase their splendor.

Incorporating gold or yellow stones like citrine in the garden can amplify the solar energies, aligning with Leo's affinity for drama and brightness.

Leo Herb Uses and Rituals: Strengthening the Heart and Spirit with Leo Herbs, Including Creative and Performance-Enhancing Applications

Leo herbs are ideal for use in practices that aim to bolster the heart, enhance creativity, and support self-expression and confidence—perfect for artists, performers, and anyone seeking to tap into their inner fire.

Creative and Heart-Strengthening Rituals:

- **Sunflower Ritual for Confidence:** Hold a few sunflower seeds in your hand while visualizing your self-esteem blossoming. Plant the seeds as a symbol of growing confidence.
- **Calendula Creativity Tea:** Sip tea made from dried calendula flowers to stimulate creative energy and bring warmth and vitality to your endeavors.
- **Saffron Elixir for Performance:** Add a few strands of saffron to a potion or elixir before an artistic performance or public speaking to enhance expressiveness and charisma.

Recipes:

- **Leo Heart Tonic:** Blend hibiscus (another heart-friendly Leo herb), calendula, and lemon balm into a tea that promotes cardiovascular health and emotional warmth.
- **Sunflower Seed Spread:** Process sunflower seeds with garlic, lemon juice, and olive oil for a nutritious spread that embodies Leo's vigor and strength.

Through these practices, "AstroHerbology: The Sky and The Soil" invites readers to harness the dynamic and radiant energy of Leo, enhancing their creative expressions and nurturing their hearts and spirits with the bold, sun-like qualities of Leo herbs. This chapter not only enriches the herbalist's repertoire but also inspires all who seek to live passionately and vibrantly, true to the spirit of Leo.

Side Note: For Saffron, please eat in moderation, if you have a sensitivity Kidney or Damaged Kidney, it is not recommended to eat Saffron, because it can lead to Urinary Infection. If you are however, on a specific Diet, please see "The Kidney Friendly Diet" that I wrote.

Thank you.

Matthew Petchinsky

If you want to see some amazing products, please visit my Virtual Dispensary: https://shift.store/sg1fan23477/retail

Chapter 7: Virgo and the Earth of Healing

Virgo, ruled by Mercury, represents precision, meticulousness, and a focus on health and wellness. Herbs associated with Virgo typically embody these qualities, offering medicinal properties that are especially effective in promoting health and hygiene. This chapter explores the properties of Virgo-associated herbs, details the precision required in cultivating them, and examines their practical uses in daily rituals for maintaining health and enhancing wellness.

Virgo Herbs Overview: Detailed Look at Virgo's Healing Herbs and Their Meticulous Properties

Herbs that resonate with Virgo are often characterized by their detailed and complex constituents that are particularly beneficial for health, hygiene, and healing. These herbs are typically used in remedies that require precise dosages and have specific applications, reflecting Virgo's association with meticulous analysis and care.

Key Virgo Herbs:

- **Echinacea:** Known for its immune-boosting properties, Echinacea is a perfect example of Virgo's focus on health maintenance and disease prevention.
- **Mint:** With its clean, crisp aroma and digestive benefits, mint is used for its hygiene-promoting properties and its meticulous ability to soothe various stomach ailments.
- **Plantain:** Often found in lawns and gardens, plantain is a potent healing herb used for its antibacterial and anti-inflammatory properties, ideal for detailed, targeted treatments.

These herbs are not only potent in their healing abilities but also require a detailed understanding to be used effectively, mirroring the analytical nature of Virgo.

Cultivating Virgo Herbs: Guidelines for Precise and Methodical Gardening Techniques Suited to Virgo Herbs

The cultivation of Virgo-associated herbs requires a level of precision and care that reflects the sign's meticulous and orderly nature. These herbs often thrive under conditions that mimic their need for cleanliness and detail.

Cultivation Tips:

- **Soil Preparation:** Virgo herbs benefit from soil that is clean and free of weeds, which can compete for nutrients and space. Incorporating plenty of organic matter can improve soil structure and nutrient content.
- **Plant Spacing:** Precise spacing is crucial to avoid overcrowding and ensure optimal growth conditions. This aligns with Virgo's need for order and efficiency.
- **Pest Management:** Implementing a regular schedule for natural pest control reflects Virgo's focus on health and purity. Using natural pest deterrents like neem oil or garlic spray helps maintain the health of the herbs without the use of harsh chemicals.

Methodical care, including regular monitoring and adjustments to cultivation practices, ensures that Virgo herbs develop their best medicinal qualities.

Virgo Herb Uses and Rituals: Practical Uses of Virgo Herbs in Health, Hygiene, and Daily Rituals for Wellness

The practical applications of Virgo herbs are vast, particularly in the realms of health maintenance, hygiene, and systematic healing practices.

Health and Hygiene Rituals:

- **Echinacea Immune Support Tincture:** Create a tincture using Echinacea to take during flu season or when feeling under the weather to boost the immune system.
- **Mint Hygiene Rinse:** Use a decoction of mint leaves as a mouthwash for its antiseptic properties, promoting oral hygiene and health.
- **Plantain Healing Poultice:** Apply a poultice of crushed plantain leaves to wounds or insect bites to reduce inflammation and prevent infection.

Daily Wellness Rituals:

- **Virgo Herbal Tea Blend:** Combine mint, chamomile (another Virgo herb), and fennel seeds to make a digestive tea that soothes the stomach and calms the nerves.
- **Daily Health Tonic:** Mix a blend of Virgo herbs like echinacea, mint, and plantain with apple cider vinegar to create a health tonic that can be taken daily to maintain wellness and vitality.

Through these practices, "AstroHerbology: The Sky and The Soil" empowers readers to incorporate Virgo herbs into their daily lives, enhancing health, promoting meticulous care, and supporting a systematic approach to wellness. This chapter not only deepens the herbalist's practice but also inspires all to embrace Virgo's detailed-oriented approach to health and hygiene in everyday life.

If you want to see some amazing products, please visit my Virtual Dispensary: https://shift.store/sg1fan23477/retail

Chapter 8: Libra and the Air of Harmony

Libra, governed by Venus, epitomizes balance, harmony, and the fostering of relationships. This sign's influence extends to a group of herbs that not only possess aesthetic beauty but also facilitate peace, balance, and improved interpersonal dynamics. This chapter delves into the characteristics of herbs associated with Libra, explores how to cultivate them in a way that harmonizes garden aesthetics with the plants' needs, and discusses their uses in rituals and applications designed to enhance balance and peace.

Libra Herbs Overview: Herbs that Embody Libra's Balance and Harmony, Ruled by Venus

Herbs resonating with Libra typically feature properties that promote balance and calm, reflecting Libra's quest for equilibrium and pleasant interactions. These plants often have beautiful flowers or pleasing aromas, underscoring Venus's influence on beauty and attraction.

Key Libra Herbs:

- **Rose:** As a symbol of love and beauty, roses are quintessentially Libran. They help soothe the heart's troubles and encourage affectionate feelings.
- **Lavender:** Known for its calming scent, lavender promotes relaxation and balance, making it ideal for maintaining Libra's harmonious vibes.
- **Spearmint:** This herb is used for its gentle, cooling properties, which align with Libra's need for mildness and its ability to smooth over conflicts.

These herbs are not only beneficial for their physical and aesthetic qualities but also for their ability to create a peaceful and harmonious environment.

Cultivating Libra Herbs: Balancing Garden Aesthetics and Plant Needs in the Cultivation of Libra Herbs

Growing Libra-associated herbs requires an approach that balances the garden's visual appeal with the practical needs of the plants, reflecting Libra's inherent desire for beauty and functionality.

Cultivation Tips:

- **Garden Design:** Arrange Libra herbs aesthetically by considering color schemes and bloom times to ensure continuous beauty throughout the growing season. This approach appeals to Libra's love for visual harmony.
- **Soil and Sunlight:** Libra herbs generally prefer well-drained soil and moderate sunlight. Ensure that areas with partial shade are utilized to cultivate herbs like lavender, which benefit from protection against harsh afternoon sun.
- **Companion Planting:** Implement companion planting to not only enhance the garden's beauty but also to promote beneficial interactions among the herbs, mirroring Libra's focus on positive relationships.

Balancing these elements in the garden fosters an environment that is as functional as it is beautiful, much like the essence of Libra.

Libra Herb Uses and Rituals: Promoting Balance, Peace, and Relationships Through Libra Herb Applications

Libra herbs are particularly effective in practices aimed at enhancing peace, resolving conflicts, and fostering better relationships, both personally and communally.

Balance and Peace Rituals:

- **Lavender Harmony Mist:** Create a mist using lavender essential oil and distilled water. Use it in your living or workspace to promote calmness and balance, essential for maintaining Libra-like harmony.
- **Rose Love Bath:** Bathe in water infused with rose petals to encourage self-love and attract romantic attention, fostering relationships in true Libran style.

Relationship Enhancing Rituals:

- **Spearmint Relationship Tea:** Brew tea with spearmint leaves to cool down heated emotions and promote understanding and patience in conversations and negotiations.
- **Libra Balance Sachet:** Fill a small sachet with dried rose, lavender, and spearmint. Carry it with you or place it in areas where harmony is needed to help diffuse tension and promote peace.

Through these practices, "AstroHerbology: The Sky and The Soil" enables readers to harness the harmonizing and beautifying powers of Libra herbs, enhancing not just their gardens but also their personal and interpersonal environments. This chapter offers insights not only into the cultivation of peace-promoting herbs but also into living a more balanced and harmonious life.

If you want to see some amazing products, please visit my Virtual Dispensary: https://shift.store/sg1fan23477/retail

Chapter 9: Scorpio and the Water of Transformation

Scorpio, ruled by Pluto and traditionally by Mars, is a sign associated with depth, transformation, and the mysteries of life and death. This sign's profound influence extends to a unique group of herbs that possess powerful transformative properties, often used in healing, protective rituals, and facilitating personal metamorphosis. This chapter explores the characteristics of herbs associated with Scorpio, discusses methods for their intense and regenerative cultivation, and examines their uses in deep, transformative rituals.

Scorpio Herbs Overview: Deep, Transformative Herbs Associated with Scorpio's Watery Energy

Herbs that resonate with Scorpio are typically those with the ability to heal, protect, and transform. They often have a potent effect on the emotional and spiritual realms, reflecting Scorpio's focus on the deep and often hidden aspects of existence.

Key Scorpio Herbs:

- **Basil:** Associated with Scorpio due to its intense flavor and protective qualities, basil is used to ward off harm and purify spaces.
- **Garlic:** Known for its powerful protective properties, garlic is also a symbol of healing and purification, resonating with Scorpio's transformative energy.
- **Aloe Vera:** With its ability to heal severe wounds and regenerate the skin, aloe vera embodies Scorpio's themes of recovery and rebirth.

These herbs not only possess strong flavors or medicinal properties but also carry profound symbolic significance, often linked to protection, healing, and spiritual awakening.

Cultivating Scorpio Herbs: Intense and Regenerative
Gardening Practices for Scorpio Herbs

Cultivating Scorpio-associated herbs involves practices that reflect the sign's intense, regenerative nature, focusing on fostering resilience and transformation within the garden.

Cultivation Tips:

- **Soil Health:** Scorpio herbs thrive in rich, well-draining soil that supports their intense growth needs. Incorporating compost or manure can enhance soil fertility and mimic the regenerative qualities of Scorpio.
- **Water Management:** These herbs often require consistent moisture but with good drainage to prevent rot. This balance of water mirrors Scorpio's watery, yet potent, nature.
- **Pruning and Regeneration:** Regular pruning of these herbs encourages regeneration and growth, symbolic of Scorpio's theme of transformation and renewal. This practice helps the plants focus their energy on producing vibrant, potent new growth.

Implementing these techniques ensures that the garden not only sustains but also regenerates, echoing the cycle of death and rebirth that is central to Scorpio's symbolism.

Scorpio Herb Uses and Rituals: Uses of Scorpio Herbs
in Rituals for Healing, Protection, and Personal
Transformation

Scorpio herbs are particularly powerful in rituals aimed at deep emotional and spiritual healing, protection against negative energies, and facilitating personal transformation.

Healing and Protection Rituals:

- **Basil Protection Spray:** Create a basil-infused water to spritz around your home or workspace to protect against negative energies and purify the environment.
- **Garlic Protective Amulet:** Hang cloves of garlic in doorways or carry them with you to ward off psychic vampires and promote spiritual healing.

Personal Transformation Rituals:

- **Aloe Vera Rebirth Mask:** Apply fresh aloe vera gel as a face mask to support skin regeneration and symbolize personal renewal and recovery.
- **Scorpio Transformation Tea:** Brew a tea with basil, mint (another Scorpio-associated herb), and a hint of garlic to drink during times of personal upheaval or transformation, supporting resilience and renewal.

Through these practices, "AstroHerbology: The Sky and The Soil" invites readers to delve into the profound and transformative powers of Scorpio herbs, enhancing not just physical health but also fostering deep spiritual and emotional growth. This chapter not only provides insights into growing these powerful plants but also offers tools for personal and spiritual transformation, embodying the true essence of Scorpio.

If you want to see some amazing products, please visit my Virtual Dispensary: https://shift.store/sg1fan23477/retail

Chapter 10: Sagittarius and the Fire of Exploration

Sagittarius, ruled by Jupiter, is the sign of exploration, adventure, and the pursuit of knowledge. This sign's influence permeates a variety of herbs that embody the expansive and philosophical nature of Sagittarius, offering benefits that enhance travel, stimulate the mind, and support spiritual growth. This chapter explores the characteristics of herbs associated with Sagittarius, discusses how to cultivate them in a manner that encourages their adventurous spirit, and delves into their uses in rituals aimed at enhancing journeys, learning experiences, and spiritual quests.

Sagittarius Herbs Overview: Herbs that Capture Sagittarius' Adventurous Spirit and Philosophical Mind

Herbs linked with Sagittarius often possess properties that stimulate the mind, enhance physical stamina, and support spiritual exploration. These herbs are robust, often large, and fast-growing, reflecting the expansive influence of Jupiter.

Key Sagittarius Herbs:

- **Sage:** Known for its wisdom-enhancing properties, sage is a quintessential Sagittarian herb that supports both intellectual and spiritual pursuits.
- **Dandelion:** As a symbol of physical and emotional resilience, dandelion promotes liver health, which in traditional medicine is often linked to the energy of adventure and travel.
- **Turmeric:** This herb is revered for its anti-inflammatory properties and its spiritual significance in rituals, embodying Sagittarius' quest for both physical and spiritual exploration.

These herbs not only promote health and wisdom but also encapsulate the essence of Sagittarius's quest for growth and expansion.

Cultivating Sagittarius Herbs: Expansive Gardening Practices That Encourage Growth and Exploration

Growing Sagittarius-associated herbs involves practices that enhance their natural tendency towards growth and exploration, mirroring the expansive nature of Sagittarius.

Cultivation Tips:

- **Space to Grow:** Sagittarius herbs typically require more space due to their expansive growth habits. Allocate ample room in the garden to allow them to thrive without constraints.
- **Soil and Fertilization:** These herbs benefit from rich, well-drained soil enhanced with organic matter or compost to support their vigorous growth.
- **Sun Exposure:** Most Sagittarius herbs thrive in full sun, which fuels their growth and potency. Ensure they receive plenty of sunlight to embody the fiery energy of Sagittarius.

Adopting these gardening practices encourages the herbs to reach their full potential, fostering a garden environment that is as adventurous and expansive as Sagittarius itself.

Sagittarius Herb Uses and Rituals: Enhancing Travel, Learning, and Spiritual Quests with Sagittarius Herbs

Sagittarius herbs are ideal for use in applications that enhance travel experiences, stimulate learning, and support spiritual exploration.

Travel and Learning Rituals:

- **Sage Travel Protection Sachet:** Carry a sachet filled with dried sage leaves when traveling to ensure safety and to heighten awareness and wisdom during your journeys.
- **Dandelion Tonic for Adventurers:** Prepare a tonic from dandelion roots to promote digestive health and vitality during travels, reflecting Sagittarius's robust nature.

Spiritual Exploration Rituals:

- **Turmeric Enlightenment Paste:** Use turmeric paste on the forehead or in meditation rituals to enhance spiritual insight and connection, tapping into Sagittarius's philosophical energy.
- **Sagittarius Spiritual Tea:** Brew a tea with sage, dandelion, and a pinch of turmeric to drink before engaging in spiritual practices or philosophical studies to enhance understanding and enlightenment.

Through these practices, "AstroHerbology: The Sky and The Soil" invites readers to embrace the adventurous and expansive qualities of Sagittarius in their herbal applications and daily rituals. This chapter not only offers practical advice on cultivating these dynamic herbs but also provides innovative ways to integrate their expansive properties into everyday life, enhancing travel, learning, and spiritual growth.

If you want to see some amazing products, please visit my Virtual Dispensary: https://shift.store/sg1fan23477/retail

Chapter 11: Capricorn and the Earth of Structure

Capricorn, ruled by Saturn, epitomizes discipline, structure, and ambition. This sign influences a variety of herbs that embody endurance, resilience, and practical utility, reflecting Capricorn's connection to the earth element and its structured nature. This chapter explores the characteristics of herbs associated with Capricorn, details methods for their cultivation that align with Capricorn's disciplined approach, and examines their uses in rituals aimed at strengthening personal structure, enhancing discipline, and promoting material success.

Capricorn Herbs Overview: Hardy Herbs that Resonate with Capricorn's Disciplined and Ambitious Nature

Herbs linked with Capricorn are typically robust, enduring, and often have strong structural qualities. These plants not only withstand harsh conditions but also offer substantial practical benefits, mirroring Capricorn's focus on utility and resilience.

Key Capricorn Herbs:

- **Comfrey:** Known for its healing properties, particularly in mending bones and wounds, comfrey reflects Capricorn's theme of structure and rebuilding.
- **Thyme:** This herb is highly resilient, thriving in less fertile soils and requiring little care once established, symbolizing Capricorn's endurance and self-sufficiency.
- **Horsetail:** Rich in silica, which is essential for strong bones and connective tissues, horsetail aligns with Capricorn's skeletal associations.

These herbs are valued not only for their medicinal properties but also for their embodiment of Capricorn's strength and persistence.

Cultivating Capricorn Herbs: Structured and Time-Tested
Approaches to Growing Capricorn-associated Herbs

The cultivation of Capricorn-associated herbs benefits from structured, methodical practices that reflect the sign's disciplined nature. These plants often thrive under conditions that mimic the serious and enduring qualities of Capricorn.

Cultivation Tips:

- **Soil Preparation:** Capricorn herbs often prosper in rocky or sandy soil, which ensures good drainage. Preparing the soil with adequate grit and minimal organic matter can mimic their natural growing conditions.
- **Climate Considerations:** These herbs generally tolerate colder, dryer climates well, reflecting Capricorn's ability to endure and thrive in challenging conditions.
- **Pruning and Maintenance:** Regular, scheduled maintenance and pruning help maintain the health and structural integrity of these plants, emphasizing Capricorn's theme of order and discipline.

Adhering to these cultivation practices ensures robust growth and maximizes the medicinal qualities of the herbs, fostering a garden that reflects Capricorn's structured and efficient approach.

Capricorn Herb Uses and Rituals: Strengthening Structure,
Discipline, and Material Success through Capricorn Herbs

Capricorn herbs are particularly effective in rituals and applications aimed at enhancing personal discipline, strengthening structure in life, and fostering material and professional success.

Structuring and Discipline Rituals:

- **Comfrey Root Wrap:** Use comfrey root in a poultice or wrap to aid in healing broken bones or sprains, symbolizing physical and metaphorical rebuilding.
- **Thyme Discipline Oil:** Infuse oil with thyme to anoint yourself when seeking to instill discipline and focus in personal or professional endeavors.

Success and Achievement Rituals:

- **Horsetail Prosperity Bag:** Carry a small bag filled with dried horsetail to promote financial stability and success, reflecting Capricorn's material ambition.
- **Capricorn Achievement Incense:** Burn an incense blend of thyme, comfrey, and cedarwood during work or study sessions to enhance concentration and fortify commitment to tasks.

Through these practices, "AstroHerbology: The Sky and The Soil" enables readers to tap into the solid, enduring qualities of Capricorn in their herbal craft and daily rituals. This chapter not only provides insights into cultivating these powerful herbs but also offers practical ways to integrate their grounding properties into life, enhancing personal discipline, structure, and success in various endeavors.

If you want to see some amazing products, please visit my Virtual Dispensary: https://shift.store/sg1fan23477/retail

Chapter 12: Aquarius and the Air of Innovation

Aquarius, ruled by Uranus, is known for its forward-thinking, innovation, and a strong sense of community. Herbs associated with this air sign often possess unique, sometimes unconventional properties that reflect Aquarius's eccentric and visionary qualities. This chapter delves into the nature of Aquarius herbs, discusses innovative approaches to their cultivation, and explores their uses in promoting community bonds, innovation, and visionary thinking.

Aquarius Herbs Overview: Unconventional Herbs Linked with Aquarius' Innovative and Eccentric Energy

Herbs that resonate with Aquarius tend to stand out for their unusual uses or growing habits. These plants often have surprising medicinal benefits and can be used in unconventional ways, mirroring the inventive and progressive spirit of Aquarius.

Key Aquarius Herbs:

- **Lemon Balm:** Known for its calming effects, lemon balm also supports cognitive function and mental clarity, reflecting Aquarius's association with intellect and mental acuity.
- **Ginkgo Biloba:** As one of the oldest living tree species, ginkgo is a symbol of longevity and resilience. It is renowned for its benefits to brain health and circulation, embodying the Aquarian ideal of breakthrough and advancement.
- **Kava Kava:** Used for its sedative and euphoric properties, Kava supports social interaction and community bonding, aligning with Aquarius's focus on social structures and humanitarian concerns.

These herbs are not only practical in their applications but also serve as botanical representations of Aquarius's affinity for innovation and social well-being.

Cultivating Aquarius Herbs: Experimental and Forward-Thinking Gardening Techniques for Aquarius Herbs

Growing Aquarius-associated herbs benefits from adopting unconventional and experimental gardening practices that resonate with Aquarius's innovative essence.

Cultivation Tips:

- **Hydroponics and Aquaponics:** Aquarius herbs thrive under innovative cultivation methods such as hydroponics or aquaponics, which conserve water and space, reflecting Aquarius's concern for the future and sustainability.
- **Companion Planting:** Implementing companion planting can enhance biodiversity and is in line with Aquarius's love for community and mutual support among different species.
- **Climate Adaptation:** Given Aquarius's association with forward-thinking, selecting and adapting these herbs to various climate conditions can be a reflection of agricultural innovation.

Utilizing these advanced techniques not only facilitates the growth of Aquarius herbs but also aligns the garden with Aquarian values of progress and ecological awareness.

Aquarius Herb Uses and Rituals: Fostering Community, Innovation, and Visionary Thinking with Aquarius Herbs

Aquarius herbs are especially potent in applications that enhance community interactions, foster innovation, and support visionary projects.

Community and Innovation Rituals:

- **Lemon Balm Community Tea:** Share a pot of lemon balm tea during community meetings or gatherings to enhance harmony and collective brainstorming.
- **Ginkgo Clarity Tincture:** Use ginkgo biloba in a tincture to promote clear thinking and vision, ideal for planning and executing innovative projects.

Visionary and Humanitarian Uses:

- **Kava Kava Social Drink:** Prepare a kava kava beverage to facilitate open and empathetic communication in social settings, encouraging Aquarian ideals of friendship and equality.
- **Aquarian Vision Incense:** Create an incense blend using lemon balm, ginkgo, and a hint of peppermint to stimulate the mind during sessions of planning or creative brainstorming.

Through these practices, "AstroHerbology: The Sky and The Soil" invites readers to embrace the inventive, communal, and progressive qualities of Aquarius in their herbal applications and daily rituals. This chapter not only offers innovative cultivation advice but also provides unique ways to integrate the visionary and humanitarian aspects of Aquarius into everyday life, enhancing community bonds and fostering an environment ripe for breakthroughs.

If you want to see some amazing products, please visit my Virtual Dispensary: https://shift.store/sg1fan23477/retail

Chapter 13: Pisces and the Water of Intuition

Pisces, ruled by Neptune and traditionally by Jupiter, is the sign associated with empathy, intuition, and the mystical aspects of the human experience. This water sign influences a variety of herbs that embody these ethereal and spiritual qualities. This chapter explores herbs aligned with Pisces' dreamy and intuitive nature, introduces fluid and intuitive practices for cultivating these herbs, and delves into their uses in rituals aimed at enhancing spiritual awareness, artistic inspiration, and emotional healing.

Pisces Herbs Overview: Dreamy, Intuitive Herbs that Align with Pisces' Empathetic and Mystical Nature

Herbs associated with Pisces typically have soothing, sedative qualities and are often used in spiritual practices to enhance intuition and connect with the higher self. These plants can also aid in healing emotional wounds and fostering compassion.

Key Pisces Herbs:

- **Lavender:** Known for its calming effects, lavender helps to soothe the mind and spirit, enhancing meditative and sleep practices.
- **Lotus:** Often used in spiritual rituals, the lotus is a symbol of purity and spiritual awakening, deeply connected to Piscean themes of transcendence and enlightenment.
- **Chamomile:** With its gentle sedative effects, chamomile aids in emotional soothing and is used for its ability to calm nervous system disturbances.

These herbs not only offer physical and emotional relief but also provide spiritual upliftment, echoing Pisces' deep connection to the ethereal realms.

Cultivating Pisces Herbs: Intuitive and Fluid Gardening Practices that Resonate with the Water Sign of Pisces

Cultivating Pisces-associated herbs calls for a gardening approach that mirrors the sign's fluidity and intuitive nature, focusing on creating a harmonious and spiritually enriching environment.

Cultivation Tips:

- **Water Features:** Incorporating elements like birdbaths, fountains, or small ponds can enhance the moisture-loving nature of Pisces herbs and create a tranquil garden atmosphere.
- **Soil Moisture:** Maintaining consistently moist soil is crucial for Pisces herbs, which thrive in lush, water-retentive environments. Mulching can help retain soil moisture and provide a nurturing ground cover.
- **Intuitive Planting:** Pisces gardeners are encouraged to follow their intuition when planting and caring for these herbs, tuning into the needs of their plants and adjusting care practices based on their observations and feelings.

These cultivation methods not only support the growth of Pisces herbs but also turn the garden into a reflective and serene space, suitable for meditation and spiritual activities.

Pisces Herb Uses and Rituals: Spiritual, Artistic, and Healing Applications of Pisces Herbs, Enhancing Intuition and Emotional Connection

Pisces herbs are particularly potent in enhancing spiritual awareness, fostering artistic inspiration, and promoting deep emotional healing.

Spiritual and Artistic Rituals:

- **Lavender Dream Pillow:** Fill a small pillow with dried lavender to promote peaceful sleep and dream inspiration, enhancing artistic vision and intuitive insight.
- **Lotus Meditation Incense:** Burn lotus incense during meditation to deepen spiritual connections and encourage states of higher consciousness.

Healing and Emotional Connection Uses:

- **Chamomile Emotional Soothe Tea:** Brew a pot of chamomile tea to help smooth emotional edges, particularly useful during times of stress or emotional upheaval.
- **Pisces Healing Bath:** Create a ritual bath with lavender, chamomile, and a few drops of eucalyptus oil to promote emotional release and deep relaxation.

Through these practices, "AstroHerbology: The Sky and The Soil" empowers readers to explore the depth of Pisces' emotional and spiritual waters, using these dreamy herbs to enhance intuition, promote healing, and connect more deeply with the artistic and mystical aspects of life. This chapter not only provides practical guidance on growing these spiritual herbs but also offers transformative ways to integrate their soothing and enlightening properties into everyday life.

If you want to see some amazing products, please visit my Virtual Dispensary: https://shift.store/sg1fan23477/retail

Conclusion: Weaving the Tapestry of the Cosmos and the Soil

As we conclude our journey through the rich and varied landscape of AstroHerbology, we are reminded of the profound interconnections between the cosmos and the soil. This ancient wisdom, once the bedrock of many traditional cultures, offers not only a deeper understanding of the natural world but also practical insights into living more harmoniously within it. This final chapter seeks to integrate the teachings of AstroHerbology into everyday life, encourage ongoing exploration and documentation, and provide directions for further study and deeper engagement with this fascinating field.

Integrating AstroHerbology into Daily Life: Practical Advice for Incorporating Astrological and Herbal Wisdom into Everyday Practices

AstroHerbology can be woven into daily life through simple, meaningful practices that enhance wellbeing, deepen our connection to the environment, and enrich our understanding of the natural cycles.

Practical Integration Tips:

- **Daily Rituals:** Start the day with a herbal tea that aligns with the astrological energy of the day. For example, sip chamomile tea on a Moon-ruled Monday to enhance calmness and intuition.
- **Gardening by the Moon:** Plan your gardening activities according to the moon phases. Plant and transplant during the waxing moon when the sap flow is increasing for optimal growth.
- **Seasonal Celebrations:** Align your celebrations and rituals with the astrological seasons. Celebrate the start of Aries with a festival of new beginnings, planting seeds both literal and metaphorical.

Incorporating these practices not only brings the power of astrological timing into everyday activities but also helps cultivate a living relationship with the herbs grown and used in your home.

The Cycle Continues: Encouragement to Observe, Document, and Learn from the Ongoing Relationship Between the Stars and the Soil

The study of AstroHerbology is cyclical and observational, requiring a commitment to learning and adapting as the cycles of life unfold.

Continual Learning and Observation:

- **Journal Keeping:** Maintain a garden journal documenting the astrological conditions, planting dates, growth observations, and herbal efficacy. This record will be invaluable for understanding the unique interactions in your environment.
- **Phenology:** Engage with the practice of phenology by noting the timing of natural occurrences such as bird migrations, flowering dates, and seasonal changes, and relate these to astrological events.
- **Community Sharing:** Participate in or form community groups focused on AstroHerbology where experiences, seeds, and herbal preparations can be shared. This fosters a wider understanding and appreciation of plant energies and celestial influences.

Further Resources: Directing Readers to Additional Sources of Information on Astrology, Herbology, and Gardening

To deepen understanding and expand knowledge, a variety of resources are available that can illuminate different aspects of Astro-Herbology.

Recommended Resources:

- **Books and Publications:** Seek out books that specialize not only in astrology and herbology but also those that explore the historical and cultural contexts of these practices.
- **Online Courses and Workshops:** Many institutions and independent educators offer courses in astrology and herbal medicine, which often include segments on their interconnections.
- **Herbal Gardens and Astrological Retreats:** Visiting herbal gardens and participating in workshops held in astrologically significant locations can provide practical and immersive learning experiences.

In guiding you through the detailed connections between the stars and the soil, "AstroHerbology: The Sky and The Soil" hopes to inspire a new appreciation for the intricate dance of the cosmos and how it can be reflected in the herbs we grow and use. By embracing these practices, readers are encouraged to foster a deeper connection with the natural world, enhancing both personal and planetary well-being. As you continue on your journey, remember that each plant, each star, each season brings new opportunities for discovery and connection, continually weaving the ever-expanding tapestry of life.

-
-
-
-
-
-
-
-
-
-

Appendix

Resources for "AstroHerbology: The Sky and The Soil"

1. Books and Publications

Books and scholarly publications are indispensable resources for those wishing to deepen their understanding of AstroHerbology. They provide foundational knowledge, historical context, and advanced methodologies that bridge astrology with the practice of herbalism.

- **Astrological Herbalism Series**: This collection of books explores the rich intersection between astrology and herbal medicine across various traditions. Each volume focuses on different aspects of AstroHerbology, such as planetary influences on herbology, historical practices across different cultures, and practical applications in modern healing arts.
- **"The Complete Guide to Astrological Self-Care" by Stephanie Marango**: This book offers a comprehensive exploration of how astrological influences affect personal health and well-being. It includes detailed sections on how to use herbs in daily routines, aligning herbal remedies with astrological cycles for maximum benefit. The guide is perfect for anyone from beginners to advanced practitioners looking to integrate more holistic practices into their self-care regimen.
- **"Herbs of the Zodiac" by Ada Muir**: Ada Muir provides an insightful exploration into the herbs associated with each zodiac sign, detailing their traditional uses, medicinal properties, and astrological significance. This book serves as an excellent reference for both astrologers and herbalists who seek to understand the vibrational qualities of herbs in relation to the astrological signs.

2. Online Platforms

The internet offers a wealth of information and interactive resources that can enhance one's practice of AstroHerbology from anywhere in the world.

- **Mountain Rose Herbs**: This website is a comprehensive resource for anyone interested in purchasing high-quality, organic herbs. It also offers extensive educational materials, including articles, blogs, and videos about herbalism, sustainable sourcing, and the therapeutic uses of herbs. The platform is particularly useful for AstroHerbologists seeking ethically sourced and energetically potent botanicals.
- **The Herbal Academy**: Known for its wide range of courses, The Herbal Academy covers topics from introductory to advanced herbal studies, often weaving in elements of plant energetics and astrological influences. Their programs are designed to cater to a variety of learning needs, from amateur gardeners to professional herbalists, and include modules specifically on incorporating astrological insights into herbal practices.
- **Astrodienst**: As a leading provider of free and comprehensive astrological charts, Astrodienst is an invaluable tool for calculating precise planetary positions and movements. This platform is essential for practitioners who need accurate astrological data to align their herbal practices with specific celestial timings.

3. Local and Global Communities

Engaging with like-minded individuals can provide support, deepen understanding, and expand the practice of AstroHerbology through shared experiences and knowledge.

- **Herb Gardens and Astrology Groups**: Many local community centers, botanical gardens, and colleges host groups and clubs that focus on the integration of gardening, herbalism, and astrology. These groups often hold regular meetings, talks, and plant walks, which are fantastic for networking and learning from peers and experts in the field.
- **Workshops and Retreats**: For those looking to immerse themselves in AstroHerbology, attending annual workshops and retreats can be particularly enriching. These events are often held in locations with natural astrological significance, such as alignment with ley lines or during specific celestial events. They offer hands-on experiences in herbal identification, cultivation, and usage, aligned with astrological teachings.

These resources collectively offer a robust framework for anyone interested in exploring and practicing AstroHerbology. By engaging with these books, online platforms, and community resources, practitioners can expand their knowledge and skills, ultimately enhancing their connection to both the cosmos and the soil.

Glossary for "AstroHerbology: The Sky and The Soil"

This glossary serves as a comprehensive resource for readers, offering detailed explanations of key terms used throughout the book. Understanding these concepts is crucial for practicing AstroHerbology effectively and integrating its principles into daily life.

- **Astrological Herbalism**: This is the practice of aligning herbal medicine with the astrological influences of planets and the zodiac. Practitioners of Astrological Herbalism use this alignment to enhance the therapeutic and magical properties of herbs. This approach combines ancient astrological knowledge with traditional herbalism to tailor treatments that are harmonized with cosmic energies, aiming to optimize healing outcomes and harness the specific powers attributed to planetary alignments and zodiacal traits.

- **Energetics**: In the context of herbal medicine, energetics refers to a classification system that describes the fundamental properties of herbs according to their perceived thermal and moisture effects on the body. These properties include hot, cold, dry, and moist. Herbal energetics are a cornerstone in many traditional healing systems, such as Ayurveda and Traditional Chinese Medicine, where herbs are selected not only for their medicinal properties but also for their ability to balance the body's internal energies and humors.

- **Mutable Signs**: In astrology, mutable signs are those that correspond to the end of each season and include Gemini (air), Virgo (earth), Sagittarius (fire), and Pisces (water). These signs are characterized by adaptability, flexibility, and change. Mutable signs are considered versatile and capable of adjusting to different circumstances, which makes them resourceful and open to change. In the context of AstroHerbology, plants associated with mutable signs often share these adaptive and transitional qualities, making them particularly useful in therapies aimed at facilitating change and adjustment in individuals.

- **Phenology**: Phenology is the scientific study of periodic biological events in the natural world as they relate to the climate and seasonal changes. In the practice of AstroHerbology, phenology is critical for determining the optimal times for planting, harvesting, and utilizing plants in accordance with both terrestrial and celestial cycles. By observing and documenting the timing of phenomena such as plant bud bursts, flowering, and animal migration patterns, practitioners can align their herbal practices with the natural rhythms of the Earth and the cosmos.

Understanding these terms enriches the reader's ability to engage deeply with the concepts presented in "AstroHerbology: The Sky and The Soil," facilitating a more informed and effective practice.

Herb Gallery for "AstroHerbology: The Sky and The Soil"

The Herb Gallery in "AstroHerbology: The Sky and The Soil" is a meticulously curated section designed to visually and intellectually engage readers by showcasing key herbs linked to each zodiac sign. This gallery provides detailed insights into the growth habits, medicinal uses, and astrological significance of each herb, accompanied by high-quality images that highlight their unique characteristics.

Featured Herbs:

- **Aries (Nettle)**: Nettle, with its sharp stingers, embodies the assertive and dynamic energy of Aries. This herb is known for its rich iron content and its ability to invigorate and energize the body. Its vigorous growth and resilience make it a perfect representative of Aries' pioneering spirit. The gallery displays nettles in various stages of growth, emphasizing their robust and hardy nature.
- **Taurus (Mint)**: Mint is associated with Taurus due to its lush, verdant growth and soothing aromatic properties, reflecting the sensual and comforting qualities of the sign. It's used both culinarily and medicinally to soothe digestive issues and calm the senses. The images show mint's vigorous spreading habit and its vibrant green leaves, which are as pleasing to the eye as to the palate.
- **Gemini (Lavender)**: Lavender's versatile uses and its ability to aid communication and calm nerves link it closely with Gemini. The herb is depicted in full bloom, highlighting its vibrant purple color, which resonates with Gemini's lively and communicative nature. The gallery explores lavender's appeal in both garden aesthetics and therapeutic contexts.

- **Cancer (Moonflower)**: Moonflower, blooming at night under the moonlight, resonates with Cancer's deep, reflective, and nurturing qualities. This night-blooming plant opens its large, fragrant flowers in the evening, symbolizing Cancer's emphasis on comfort, home, and the intuitive aspect of life. The photographs capture the ethereal beauty and transient openness of the flowers.
- **Leo (Sunflower)**: Sunflower captures Leo's bright, sunny disposition and its association with the heart and vitality. Towering and facing the sun, sunflowers are the epitome of Leo's bold and radiant energy. The gallery highlights their striking stature and the vibrant yellow petals that mimic the sun's rays.
- **Virgo (Echinacea)**: Echinacea, known for its medicinal properties, especially in enhancing immune function, correlates with Virgo's association with health and meticulous care. The images focus on the distinct conical shape of its flower heads and its robust nature, underscoring Virgo's precise and health-conscious attributes.
- **Libra (Rose)**: Roses, with their harmonious and aesthetic qualities, are linked to Libra. The gallery showcases different varieties, emphasizing the balance between their beauty and thorns, which mirrors Libra's quest for balance and fairness. The roses are displayed in a range of colors, each symbolizing different aspects of Libra's love for beauty and harmony.
- **Scorpio (Basil)**: Basil, with its intense flavor and protective qualities, is tied to Scorpio's deep, transformative energy. Its use in both culinary and magical practices to cleanse and protect makes it a suitable herb for Scorpio. The images show basil's rich, green foliage and clusters of small flowers, highlighting its robust and mysterious nature.
- **Sagittarius (Sage)**: Sage is connected to Sagittarius through its use in clearing and expanding the mind and space, reflecting Sagittarius's love for exploration and higher learning. The gallery focuses on its robust leaves and the purifying smoke produced

when burned, showcasing the herb's spiritual and philosophical significance.

- **Capricorn (Thyme)**: Thyme, known for its resilience and essential role in culinary and medicinal practices, reflects Capricorn's disciplined and foundational energy. The photographs illustrate thyme's modest yet strong presence in the garden, symbolizing Capricorn's enduring and structured nature.
- **Aquarius (Kava Kava)**: Kava Kava, used for its unique sedative and euphoric effects, aligns with Aquarius's innovative and community-oriented spirit. The gallery explores its use in social ceremonies and as a tool for mental relaxation, reflecting Aquarius's progressive and humanitarian traits.
- **Pisces (Lotus)**: Lotus, with its roots in muddy water and beautiful flowers rising above the surface, symbolizes Pisces' mystical and transcendent nature. The images capture the serene and ethereal aspect of the lotus, echoing Pisces' connection to spirituality and the collective unconscious.

This Herb Gallery not only enhances the reader's understanding of each herb's connection to astrological signs but also serves as a visual inspiration, bringing the text's descriptions to vibrant life. Through this detailed presentation, readers can better appreciate the unique contributions of each herb to the practice of AstroHerbology and find deeper connections between the cosmos and the soil.

Extensive List of Magick Books

The following collection of books provides a thorough introduction to various aspects of magic, witchcraft, and Wicca, ranging from beginner to more advanced levels. These texts offer insights into ritual practices, spellcraft, herbal magic, and the philosophical underpinnings of magical traditions. They serve as invaluable resources for anyone looking to deepen their understanding and practice of the craft.

Gavin and Yvonne Frost

- **"The Magic Power of Witchcraft" by Gavin and Yvonne Frost**: This foundational text delves into practical witchcraft techniques, including detailed instructions on how to use herbs in spells and rituals. It offers clear, step-by-step guidance suitable for beginners but also valuable to experienced practitioners.
- **"The Witch's Magical Handbook" by Gavin and Yvonne Frost**: This comprehensive guide provides techniques and spells that utilize the energies of the natural world. It includes an extensive section dedicated to the herbal correspondences for various magical practices, making it a practical resource for those interested in incorporating natural elements into their magical work.

Raymond Buckland

- **"Buckland's Complete Book of Witchcraft" by Raymond Buckland**: Often referred to as "Buckland's Big Blue," this book is one of the most widely read introductions to Wicca and modern witchcraft. It covers a broad range of topics from the history of witchcraft to practical exercises in divination, spellcasting, and herbalism.
- **"Practical Candleburning Rituals" by Raymond Buckland**: This book is a straightforward guide to performing effective spells with candles. It's an excellent resource for beginners looking to understand the basics of spellcraft and how to integrate simple candle magic into daily practices.

Scott Cunningham

- **"Wicca: A Guide for the Solitary Practitioner" by Scott Cunningham**: This is one of the best introductory books for individuals who are beginning their journey into the practice of

Wicca and witchcraft without a coven. Cunningham explains the fundamental principles and philosophies in a clear, accessible way, including how to create and perform rituals, spells, and divination.

- **"Encyclopedia of Magical Herbs" by Scott Cunningham**: An essential guide for anyone using herbs in magic, this encyclopedia provides comprehensive descriptions of herbs, including their magical properties and uses. This book is a must-have for both beginners and experienced practitioners interested in expanding their knowledge of herbal magic.

Silver RavenWolf

- **"To Ride A Silver Broomstick: New Generation Witchcraft" by Silver RavenWolf**: This book offers a fresh, accessible perspective on modern witchcraft, blending tradition with contemporary insights. It's particularly appealing for younger readers and beginners and covers a wide range of topics, including the Internet's role in modern witchcraft.
- **"Solitary Witch: The Ultimate Book of Shadows for the New Generation" by Silver RavenWolf**: This extensive guide serves as a comprehensive Book of Shadows that includes everything a new or solitary practitioner might need to know, from Sabbats and Esbats to magical recipes, tarot spreads, and detailed information on herbs.

These books collectively provide a robust foundation for understanding and practicing magic and witchcraft, with a special focus on the integration of herbal knowledge into magical practices. Whether you are just starting out or looking to deepen your existing practice, these resources offer valuable guidance and inspiration.

Message from the Author: I personally know of thes authors, I have several books from Cunningham and Buckland. I have a copy of "A Witch's Magical Handbook" by Gavin and Yvonne Frost, it is one of my favorites.

Personally though, I would not recommend Silver Ravenwolf, her style of write is more of trying to make you feel bad for what is know to all Witches as "The Burning Times". Her style of writing tries to guilt trip, rather than teach, please chose wisely, thank you.

Matthew Petchinsky

Herb Horoscope: Astrological Guide to Planting, Harvesting, and Using Herbs

This herb horoscope provides a structured approach to integrating the wisdom of astrology with the practice of herbalism. Each zodiac sign is matched with a corresponding herb that reflects the sign's intrinsic qualities. The guide includes the best times for planting and harvesting these herbs based on lunar cycles and planetary alignments, as well as their specific medicinal and magical uses.

Aries

- **Herb:** Nettle

- **Planting and Harvesting Times:** Plant during the first quarter moon in Aries for optimal growth. Harvest when Mars is strong and well-aspected, ideally when the moon is in Aries or Scorpio.
- **Herbal Uses:** Medicinally, nettle is used to stimulate metabolism and treat iron deficiency, mirroring Aries' energetic and pioneering spirit. Magically, it can be used for protection and to bolster courage.

Taurus

- **Herb:** Mint
- **Planting and Harvesting Times:** Plant during the full moon in Taurus to enhance growth and flavor. Harvest during the waning moon to capture the plant's full aromatic potential.
- **Herbal Uses:** Mint is beneficial for digestion and can soothe stomach ailments, reflecting Taurus's love for food and comfort. In magic, it attracts prosperity and stability.

Gemini

- **Herb:** Lavender
- **Planting and Harvesting Times:** Plant during Gemini's waxing moon for best aromatic yields. Harvest just before the full moon to maximize essential oils and potency.
- **Herbal Uses:** Lavender aids in relaxation and promotes clear communication, perfect for social Gemini. It's used in spells to enhance eloquence and calm anxiety.

Cancer

- **Herb:** Chamomile

- **Planting and Harvesting Times:** Plant during the new moon in Cancer for a nurturing growth environment. Harvest during the full moon to capture the soothing energies of the plant.
- **Herbal Uses:** Chamomile is ideal for calming mood swings and promoting restful sleep, aligning with Cancer's need for comfort and emotional balance. Magically, it protects the home.

Leo

- **Herb:** Sunflower
- **Planting and Harvesting Times:** Sow seeds with the new moon in Leo to capture the sun's full strength as the moon waxes. Harvest when the sun is in Leo, during the daytime, to harness vibrant energy.
- **Herbal Uses:** Sunflower seeds promote vitality and are good for heart health, mirroring Leo's vibrant and hearty nature. Use in magic for fame and success.

Virgo

- **Herb:** Echinacea
- **Planting and Harvesting Times:** Plant during the waxing moon in Virgo for strong medicinal qualities. Harvest before the moon reaches full to maintain the herb's integrity.
- **Herbal Uses:** Echinacea boosts the immune system and is perfect for meticulous Virgo's focus on health. It's used in protective spells.

Libra

- **Herb:** Rose

- **Planting and Harvesting Times:** Plant during Libra's waxing moon for beautiful blooms. Harvest during the full moon to enhance the plant's aesthetic and aromatic qualities.
- **Herbal Uses:** Rose is used to soothe skin and enhance beauty, complementing Libra's appreciation for aesthetics. In magic, it's used to attract love and promote peace.

Scorpio

- **Herb:** Basil
- **Planting and Harvesting Times:** Plant basil during Scorpio's waxing moon to tap into the sign's regenerative properties. Harvest as the moon wanes to concentrate its intense flavors and medicinal properties.
- **Herbal Uses:** Basil is a powerful detoxifying herb and can be used to clear out old emotional baggage, aligning with Scorpio's transformative nature. It's used in magic for protection and exorcism.

Sagittarius

- **Herb:** Sage
- **Planting and Harvesting Times:** Plant during Sagittarius's new moon for expansion and growth. Harvest during the full moon to capture the philosophical essence of the herb.
- **Herbal Uses:** Sage enhances mental clarity and is often used for purification, reflecting Sagittarius's quest for truth and knowledge. Use in magic to promote wisdom and spiritual protection.

Capricorn

- **Herb:** Thyme

- **Planting and Harvesting Times:** Plant during the new moon in Capricorn to build strong root systems. Harvest during the full moon to solidify its robust flavor and medicinal strength.
- **Herbal Uses:** Thyme is excellent for strengthening the immune system and can aid in concentration, useful for industrious Capricorn. Magically, it fosters courage and wards off negativity.

Aquarius

- **Herb:** Kava Kava
- **Planting and Harvesting Times:** Plant during Aquarius's waxing moon to encourage social growth. Harvest during the full moon to enhance its neurological effects.
- **Herbal Uses:** Kava kava is used for its calming effects and helps promote community and communication, ideal for sociable Aquarius. Use in magic for protection and to promote emotional calm.

Pisces

- **Herb:** Lotus
- **Planting and Harvesting Times:** Plant during the waxing moon in Pisces to connect with spiritual energies. Harvest during the full moon to maximize spiritual and medicinal potency.
- **Herbal Uses:** Lotus enhances meditation and spiritual connectivity, perfect for mystical Pisces. It is used in magical practices to enhance psychic abilities and promote spiritual openings.

This herb horoscope guide helps readers align their gardening and herbal practices with the cycles of the moon and the astrological energies, maximizing the effectiveness of their efforts both in healing and magical workings.

<u>Message from the Author:</u>

I hope you enjoyed this book, I love astrology and knew there was not a book such as this out on the shelf. I love metaphysical items as well. Please check out my other books:

-Life of Government Benefits

-My life of Hell

-My life with Hydrocephalus

-Red Sky

-World Domination:Woman's rule

-World Domination:Woman's Rule 2: The War

-Life and Banishment of Apophis: book 1

-The Kidney Friendly Diet

-The Ultimate Hemp Cookbook

-Creating a Dispensary(legally)

-Cleanliness throughout life: the importance of showering from childhood to adulthood.

-Strong Roots: The Risks of Overcoddling children

-Hemp Horoscopes: Cosmic Insights and Earthly Healing

- Celestial Hemp Navigating the Zodiac: Through the Green Cosmos

-Astrological Hemp: Aligning The Stars with Earth's Ancient Herb

-The Astrological Guide to Hemp: Stars, Signs, and Sacred Leaves

-Green Growth: Innovative Marketing Strategies for your Hemp Products and Dispensary

-Cosmic Cannabis

-Astrological Munchies

-Henry The Hemp

-Zodiacal Roots: The Astrological Soul Of Hemp

- **Green Constellations: Intersection of Hemp and Zodiac**

-Hemp in The Houses: An astrological Adventure Through The Cannabis Galaxy

-Galactic Ganja Guide

Heavenly Hemp

Zodiac Leaves
Doctor Who Astrology
Cannastrology
Stellar Satvias and Cosmic Indicas
Celestial Cannabis: A Zodiac Journey
Check out my Virtual dispensary for all your hemp needs: https://shift.store/sg1fan23477/retail
If you want solar for your home go here: https://www.harborsolar.live/apophisenterprises/

Instagrams:
@apophis_enterprises,
@hempkingdom2024
@apophisbookemporium
, @apophisfashion,
@apophisscardshop
Twitter: @apophisenterpr1,
Tiktok:@apophisenterprise
Youtube: @sg1fan23477
Podcast:Apophis Chat Zone: https://open.spotify.com/show/5zXbrCLEV2xzCp8ybrfHsk?si=fb4d4fdbdce44dec
Newsletter: https://apophiss-newsletter-27c897.beehiiv.com/